To Those Who Have Gone Home Tired

# To Those Who Have Gone Home Tired
## New & Selected Poems

## W. D. Ehrhart

Thunder's Mouth Press
New York · Chicago

Design by Laurie Bolchert.

Cover photo by Eric P. Eberhardt.

Grateful acknowledgement is made to the New York State Council on the Arts and the National Endowment for the arts for financial assistance with the publication of this volume.

The selected poems in this collection were written between 1970 and 1980, and taken from the following books:

A Generation of Peace, New Voices Publishing Company, 1975 (revised and reprinted under the same title by Samisdat Press, 1977).
Rootless, Samisdat Press, 1977.
Empire, Samisdat Press, 1978.
The Samisdat Poems, Samisdat Press, 1980 (incorporating the three previous Samisdat collections plus a section of newer poems).
Matters of the Heart, Adastra Press, 1981.
Channel Fever, Backstreet Editions, 1982.

Many of the poems in A Generation of Peace, combined with several poems each from Rootless and Empire, were published under the title of The Awkward Silence by Northwoods Press in 1980.

Some of the new and previously uncollected poems first appeared in Stone Country, Friends Journal, and Asphodel.

811.54
Eh8t

Library of Congress Cataloging in Publication Data

Ehrhart, W. D. (William Daniel), 1948–
.  To those who have gone home tired.

    1. Vietnamese Conflict, 1961–1975—Poetry. 2. War poetry, American. I. Title.
PS3555.H67A6   1984        811'.54        84-91
ISBN 0-938410-22-9 (pbk.)

# Contents

## 1 from *A Generation of Peace*

## 2 from *Rootless*

# 3 from *Empire*

# 4 from *The Samisdat Poems*

# 5 from *Matters of the Heart*

# 6 from *Channel Fever*

# 7 New Poems

for Anne
for a lifetime

## One Night on Guard Duty

The first salvo is gone before I can turn,
but there is still time to see the guns
hurl a second wave of steel against the dark.

The shells arc up,
tearing through the air like some invisible hand
crinkling giant sheets of cellophane among the stars.

The night waits, breathless,
till the far horizon erupts in brilliant
pulsing silence.

# Souvenirs

"Bring me back a souvenir," the captain called.
"Sure thing," I shouted back above the amtrac's roar.

Later that day,
the column halted,
we found a Buddhist temple by the trail.
Combing through a nearby wood,
we found a heavy log as well.

It must have taken more than half an hour,
but at last we battered in
the concrete walls so badly
that the roof collapsed.

Before it did,
I took two painted vases
Buddhists use for burning incense.

One vase I kept,
and one I offered proudly to the captain.


# Farmer Nguyen

When we swept through farmer Nguyen's hamlet,
some people said that farmer Nguyen
had given rice to the Vietcong.

> You picked the wrong side, farmer Nguyen.
> We took you in, and beat you,
> and put you in a barbed wire cage.

When the Vietcong returned to farmer Nguyen's hamlet,
some people said that farmer Nguyen
had given information to the Round Eyes.

> Wrong again, farmer Nguyen.
> They took more rice, and beat you,
> and made you carry supplies.

# Sergeant Jones

And then there's Sergeant Jones.
He's hard, but knows the ways
to handle other men
when they're afraid.

Always has a good word, too.
Not just for us either—
speaks Vietnamese fluently;
makes the girls at the district office
giggle with delight
every time we go there.

The kind of guy the young enlisted men
admire:
he can hit a gook at 50 yards
with a fuckin' .45.


# The Rat

Flashing jagged teeth,
he squealed and shrieked and tried
to break the circle of our flailing rifle butts.

But he couldn't; and at last,
trapped in a corner of the bunker,
he only glared at us through wild
uncomprehending eyes.

His final glimpse of life
was the bottom of a cinderblock.


# The Sniper's Mark

He seemed in a curious hurry
to burn up what was left
of the energy inside—

A brainless, savage flurry
of arms and legs and eyes.

# Mail Call

It's strange, the obstacles
that fail to break the will:
boredom, body rot, pervasive fear of death.
Stranger still, the unanticipated breath
that tips the scales:

        Private Thomas married
only weeks before he left. Now, ten months past,
he was our point man—unscathed, unharried,
though constantly exposed. Ten months unmarked—

and over in an instant with a single shot
that punched a hole in the hot day; with Thomas,
lifeless, sprawled across his cot;
with the lawyer's note,
blood-spattered, crumpled in his fist;
with his last "I love you" trapped inside his throat
by the barrel of a pistol.

# The One That Died

You bet we'll soon forget the one that died;
he isn't welcome any more.
He could too easily take our place
for us to think about him
any longer than it takes
to sort his personal effects:
    a pack of letters,
    cigarettes,
    photos and a wallet.
We'll keep the cigarettes;
divide them up among us.
His parents have no use for them,
and cigarettes are hard to get.

# Night Patrol

Another night coats the nose and ears:
smells of fish and paddy water,
smoke from cooking fires and stale urine
drift uneasily, cloaked in silence;
the marketplace deserted, shuttered
houses, empty paths, all cloaked in silence;
shadows bristle.

Our gravel-crunching boots tear great
holes in the darkness, make us wince
with every step. A mangy dog
pits the stomach: rifles level;
nervous fingers hit the safety catch.

# The Next Step

The next step you take
may lead you into an ambush.

The next step you take
may trigger a tripwire.

The next step you take
may detonate a mine.

The next step you take
may tear your leg off at the hip.

The next step you take
may split your belly open.

The next step you take
may send a sniper's bullet through your brain.

The next step you take.
The next step you take.

The next step.
The next step.

The next step.

# Guerrilla War

It's practically impossible
to tell civilians
from the Vietcong.

Nobody wears uniforms.
They all talk
the same language,
(and you couldn't understand them
even if they didn't).

They tape grenades
inside their clothes,
and carry satchel charges
in their market baskets.

Even their women fight;
and young boys,
and girls.

It's practically impossible
to tell civilians
from the Vietcong;

after a while,
you quit trying.


# Time on Target

We used to get intelligence reports
from the Vietnamese district offices.
Every night, I'd make a list
of targets for artillery to hit.

It used to give me quite a kick
to know that I, a corporal,
could command an entire battery
to fire anywhere I said.

One day, while on patrol,
we passed the ruins of a house;
beside it sat a woman
with her left hand torn away;
beside her lay a child, dead.

When I got back to base,
I told the fellows in the COC;
it gave us all a lift to know
all those shells we fired every night
were hitting something.

# Hunting

Sighting down the long black barrel,
I wait till front and rear sights
form a perfect line on his body,
then slowly squeeze the trigger.

The thought occurs
that I have never hunted anything in my whole life
except other men.

But I have learned by now
where such thoughts lead,
and soon pass on
to chow, and sleep,
and how much longer till I change my socks.

# Christ

I saw the Crucified Christ three days ago.
He did not hang on the cross,
but lay instead on the shambled terrace
of what had been a house.
There were no nails in His limbs,
no crown of thorns, no open wounds.
The soldiers had left nothing
but a small black hole upon His cheek.
And He did not cry: "Forgive them, Lord;"
but only lay there, gazing at a monsoon sky.

Today, angelic hosts
of flies caress His brow;
and from His swollen body comes
the sweet-sick stench of rotting flesh.

# The Hawk and Two Suns

The silver hawk swoops 300 miles per hour
almost standing still,
locks his grid-coordinate prey
between his cross-haired eyes,
holds, extends twin silver talons—
cannisters that tumble through the air—
almost horizontal, they strike the ground together.

Coming from the sun, the hawk creates another sun
that spreads a brilliant orange sun-storm
that billows out and rolls along the earth;
billows, then recedes;
leaves behind burnt-black bodies and lungs
burst outward in frantic search of oxygen.

The hawk shrieks his predatory victory cry,
and wheels away to join the greater sun
he drains with every raid.


# The Generals' War

Paper orders passed down and executed:

straggling back in plum-colored rags,
one-legged, in slings, on stretchers,
in green plastic bags,
with stubbled faces
and gaunt eyes hung in sockets;

returned to paper
for some general to read about
and pin a medal to.

# The Ambush

Illusion:
waiting to come to an end.

The target:
black shape
against the bluer black of night.

Response:
extremities converge inside the chest,
burst outward through the arms,
explode
from the muzzle of an automatic rifle
toward the lurching, speechless figure
caught mid-sentence
by the fury of an inability to hate.

> (The target is a pretext;
> it has a hundred names.
> None belong to it;
> all are out of reach.)

Respite:
through the long night after,
sleep—the deep and total sleep
that swallows one whose mind is without thought,
empty, drained, at peace.

Illusion shattered:
daylight;
things remain as they were.

# Another Life

The long day's march is over.
Ten thousand meters through the bush
with flak jacket, rifle, helmet,
three hundred rounds of ammunition,
three days' rations, two canteens,
hand grenades, a cartridge belt;
pack straps grinding at the shoulders,
feet stuffed in boots that stumble forward
mile after hill after hour;
the sun a crushing hundred-and-two,
sweat in the eyes and salt on the lips;
and always aware that Charlie only waits.

The march is over for today.
Now, heaped against a paddy dike
and fighting back the sweetness of exhaustion,
I close my eyes
and struggle to recall
another life.


# Coming Home

San Francisco airport—

no more corpsmen stuffing ruptured chests
with cotton balls and not enough heat tabs
to eat a decent meal.

I asked some girl to sit
and have a coke with me.
She thought I was crazy;
I thought she was going to call a cop.

I bought a ticket for Philadelphia.
At the loading gate, they told me:
"Thank you for flying TWA;
we hope you will enjoy your flight."

No brass bands;
no flags,
no girls,
no cameramen.

Only a small boy who asked me
what the ribbons on my jacket meant.

# Old Myths

Citations, medals, warrants of promotion:

all the things I ever earned I framed
and tacked up in the attic room
I used to use for studying.

That was many years ago—
before events began to show
how deeply they were etched.

Now the room is cluttered with old clothes
and broken toys and boxes.
I don't go up there any more:
I've lived the myth, and know
what lies are made of.

Yet even now, sometimes I find
traces of an older pride:

I guess old myths die hard.

# A Relative Thing

We are the ones you sent to fight a war
you didn't know a thing about.

It didn't take us long to realize
the only land that we controlled
was covered by the bottoms of our boots.

When the newsmen said that naval ships
had shelled a VC staging point,
we saw a breastless woman
and her stillborn child.

We laughed at old men stumbling
in the dust in frenzied terror
to avoid our three-ton trucks.

We fought outnumbered in Hue City
while the ARVN soldiers looted bodies
in the safety of the rear.
The cookies from the wives of Local 104
did not soften our awareness.

We have seen the pacified supporters
of the Saigon government
sitting in their jampacked cardboard towns,
their wasted hands placed limply in their laps,
their empty bellies waiting for the rice
some district chief has sold
for profit to the Vietcong.

We have been Democracy on Zippo raids,
burning houses to the ground,
driving eager amtracs through new-sown fields.

We are the ones who have to live
with the memory that we were the instruments
of your pigeon-breasted fantasies.
We are inextricable accomplices
in this travesty of dreams:
but we are not alone.

We are the ones you sent to fight a war
you did not know a thing about—
those of us that lived
have tried to tell you what went wrong.
Now you think you do not have to listen.

Just because we will not fit
into the uniforms of photographs
of you at twenty-one
does not mean you can disown us.

We are your sons, America,
and you cannot change that.
When you awake,
we will still be here.

# Imagine

The conversation turned to Vietnam.
He'd been there, and they asked him
what it had been like:
had he been in battle?
Had he ever been afraid?

Patiently, he tried to answer
questions he had tried to answer
many times before.

They listened, and they strained
to visualize the words:
newsreels and photographs, books
and Wilfred Owen tumbled
through their minds.
Pulses quickened.

They didn't notice, as he talked,
his eyes, as he talked,
his eyes begin to focus
through the wall, at nothing,
or at something inside.

When he finished speaking,
someone asked him:
had he ever killed?

# Making the Children Behave

Do they think of me now
in those strange Asian villages
where nothing ever seemed
quite human
but myself
and my few grim friends
moving through them
hunched
in lines?

When they tell stories to their children
of the evil
that awaits misbehavior,
is it me they conjure?


# To the Asian Victors

The great miscalculation
refuses to be covered over.
I have tried every solution,
yet the paint always begins to peel
even before it is dry,
and the bare room comes back
again.

This last time
it returned as yellow frightened faces
spilling from the bellies of birds,
like splinters from old wounds
that will not heal.

In school, as a child,
I learned about Redcoats—
I studied myself,
though I did not know it at the time.
The lesson remains;
only the teacher has changed.

Looking back
at the pale shadow forever
calling at dusk from the forest,
I remember the dead, I
remember the dying.

But I cannot ever quite remember
what I went looking for,
or what it was I lost
in that alien land that became
more I
than my own can ever be again.

# To Maynard on the Long Road Home

Biking at night with no lights
and no helmet, you were struck
and hurled sixty feet,
dead on impact.
The newspapers noted the irony:
surviving the war
to die like that, alone,
on a hometown street.
I knew better.

Years before, on Christmas Day,
I met you on a road near Quang Tri;
a chance reunion of Perkasie boys
grown up together in a town
that feared God and raised sons
willing to die for their country.
"Who're you with?
Have you seen much action?
What the hell's going on here?"
All that afternoon we remembered
our shared youth: the old boat
with Jeffy and the slow leak,
skipping Sunday School to read comics
and drink orange soda at Flexer's,
the covered bridge near Bryan's farm.

Though neither of us
spoke of it, we knew then
we had lost
more than our youth.

I show my poems to friends now and then,
hoping one or two might see
my idealistic bombast
in a new light:
the sharp turns of mood, anger
defying visible foundation,
inexplicable sadness.
How often they wonder aloud
how I managed to survive—
they always assume the war is over,
not daring to imagine our wounds,
or theirs, if it is not.
I think of you,
and wonder if either of us
will ever come home.

# The Last Day

Night drifts coldly into dawn.
Stark slate turns
first grey, then red.
The sea lies flat;
the hills breathless.

Terror and alarm, confusion,
fire, death, apocalyptic change—
all these we imagined.
In the darkest alleys of our minds
we covered every possibility.

No one thought of this.

The sun climbs in the east;
still the streets and roads
are empty. No one moves;
each is locked forever

in a dream.

# The Flying Gypsy

I. Windward
She sits each night near Market Street.
And every night she wears the same
old dress and faded flowered hat
that must have fired young men's dreams
fifty years ago.
A battered Gimbels shopping bag
holds everything she owns.

II. Leeward
Once, many years ago, I came
by chance upon a clipper ship
tied up beside an unused dock.
The Flying Gypsy was her name;
and in her time, white canvas bent
before the wind, she must have been
the swiftest lady on the sea;
for even then, her rotting shrouds
and broken spars stretched anxious
fingers to the gentlest breeze.

III. Windward
I pass that way each night at ten.
No matter that I know by now,
before I see her, she'll be there;
in the quiet, empty street
her solitary presence always startles:
saying nothing, she demands her place
with eyes that stare through pounding waves,
and lips still tasting salt.

# Cathay

"Dreamers! Damn the lot of you!
You're all mad."
                          And so they were:
Gaspar and Miguel, Cabot, Grube;
dreamers all, gone
to seek that westward passage
to the pleasures of Cathay, and all,
finally, lost without a trace.

Yet who's to say
they do not lie even now
beneath a mandarin sky,
smoking from those graceful pipes,
and listening
to accomplished fingers play?

# Geese

When you went away
the leaves began to fall;
the blue sky scattered before clouds
like flustered pigeons in the plaza
and the geese by the river,
thinking winter had come,
cried out and fled.

All that day the colors
slowly drained from the world
like sand slipping through small
invisible holes in the earth.
The people lost their faces,
appearing only as bland shapes
at the end of long tunnels.

Back home I discovered
a new silence
clinging to the walls like frost.
Later the wind came around to the north,
beating at the windows,
writing your name on the rattling glass;
and I could not sleep that night.

All this was a long time ago;
but the wind still blows from the north
and the frost on the walls remains.
The colors have not returned, nor the leaves
nor the faces nor the blue sky.
And I do not wonder any longer
when they will;

I only wonder how the geese knew.

# Bicentennial

It was a hard winter,
and a harder march
before you finally rested.

The city you fled that fall
others later fled.
Still others remain—
some, like those who drove you out,
by choice; most
because they are crippled.

Our Fathers too are gone.
Imposters wear their faces.
They are clever—
many do not know the difference;
those that do
seem not to care any more.

The clever ones
dress their sons and policies
in red coats.
They arm the world,
and ride their brothers everywhere.

Up north, the tide
has long since washed the tea
from Boston harbor.
Now we have votes
which are empty.

Looking down from your encampment,
the lush green hills
give way
to belching black industrial cavities
and stark concrete gouges.
They were built
by those who line their pockets
with your blood.
They remain
because your people lack the will
to staunch your bleeding.

Rebel, it was you
who made the Revolution happen.

If you could see,
what has happened to the Revolution,
would you still be willing
to bear the long cold winter of Valley Forge
to cross the icy Delaware
to Trenton
and your death?

# Money in the Bank
## for Alfred Starr Hamilton

Sixty-one years
of your life are gone and I
have never heard of you
until today.

I understand the poems
simply grow
beneath your pillow as you sleep
in your cheap boardinghouse room,
and you only have to rise
and type them in the morning,
ten at a crack before lunch
and the daily paper you read
at the Montclair Public Library
because you cannot afford your own,
like the cigarettes
you pick up from the street.

Sixty-one years old,
and I have never heard of you
because you are not taught in school
and your poems do not appear in *Poetry*
and your only book was not reviewed
because we have no use for poets
who have no use
for us.

Well, Mr. Hamilton,
now I have heard of you;
and tomorrow the mailman
will give you this
(along perhaps with another summons
from the Garden State
because they say you are a vagrant),
and you'll open it and find
some person that you do not know
has sent you money.

I'd like to say I sent you this
because I simply care
about another human being.

But the truth is, Mr. Hamilton,
this money you receive
is for myself,
and for the future;

and I send it out of fear.

# To Those Who Have Gone Home Tired

After the streets fall silent
After the bruises and the tear-gassed eyes are healed
After the concensus has returned
After the memories of Kent and My Lai and Hiroshima
lose their power
and their connections with each other
and the sweaters labeled Made In Taiwan
After the last American dies in Canada
and the last Korean in prison
and the last Indian at Pine Ridge
After the last whale is emptied from the sea
and the last leopard emptied from its skin
and the last drop of blood refined by Exxon
After the last iron door clangs shut
behind the last conscience
and the last loaf of bread is hammered into bullets
and the bullets
scattered among the hungry

What answers will you find
What armor will protect you
when your children ask you
Why?


# Going Home with the Monkeys

Another day gone;
we go home in winter twilight,
warm in our scarves and mufflers,
counting our small accomplishments
like fingers on a hand.

We did our jobs;
we were kind today—
or if we were not,
tomorrow we can mend it.

It is evening;
we could rest—
except for the beggar on the corner,
a headline, a siren, a dream
of green palms in moonlight:

they rise up before us like wind,
like warnings,
and go away,
and rise up farther on.

They are the shadows of everything,
except what we are,
and what we have done.

And they never seem to get
any closer.

And they never leave us alone.

# Rootless

I have been walking all afternoon,
wondering how I have come to this day
already exhausted,
with nothing but holes in my pockets,
and only a handful of poems
to bind these twenty-seven years together;
trying to cling to small things
like the names of the flowers I know
or the crazy paths of butterflies,
but always returning to a woman
who told me once
I was a man
without roots—born
to the deck of a ship at midnight
or the soft purr of stars
or the cry of water searching for the sea,
but not to this world.

That woman and I made love,
our bodies slapping with desire—
but in the morning,
both of us naked,
she saw the desperation in my eyes,
and left me with her words
drumming in my ears like thunder.

I used to fear death.
Now I only fear
a slow and violent death;
and even that, I know,
will be bearable.
The hot, windless afternoon
aimlessly drifts toward evening.
In the park, a man set in stone
stares at his lengthening shadow.

# Granddad

I remember only a table,
Fig Newtons and a lap
on the porch of a house
in Asbury Park, New Jersey.
You don't even have a face then;
I found it later
in pictures.

Grandmother says you were crazy:
building railroads
and going wherever you pleased;
one job here,
another one there,
footloose half your life;
and always the opera,
and Verdi; and later,
teaching your children Italian.

She never has used
the word love
when she speaks of you.
But in spite of herself,
rumpled old Eastern Shore Scots-Irish,
she speaks with respect,
and I know she loved you.

She says I'm a lot like you.
I grow silent inside
to think of it—as though,
if I'm quiet,
I'll hear you moving
in my veins.

## The Trial

Grandfather Ehrhart
dead of the flu in 1918,
younger than I am now,
leaving a wife and two kids
on a farm in Adams County:

fifty-four years
my grandmother labored without him,
trusting in God and living to see
four grandchildren spring from his blood
to devour her cherry pies.

Strong as a willow, that woman,
bearing the winds with a whispered grace,
and the yellow blossoms with joy.

But the night he died,
a widow of twenty-five lay down
beside his body
with the promise of a lifetime
turning cold.

# Letter

## to a north Vietnamese soldier
## whose life crossed paths with mine
## in Hue City, February 5th, 1968

Thought you killed me
with that rocket? Well, you nearly did:
splattered walls and splintered air,
knocked me cold and full of holes,
and brought the roof down on my head.

But I lived,
long enough to wonder often
how you missed; long enough
to wish too many times
you hadn't.

What's it like back there?
It's all behind us here;
and after all those years of possibility,
things are back to normal.
We just had a special birthday,
and we've found again our inspiration
by recalling where we came from
and forgetting where we've been.

Oh, we're still haggling over pieces
of the lives sticking out
beyond the margins of our latest
history books—but no one haggles
with the authors.

*Do better than that*
you cockeyed gunner with the brass
to send me back alive among a people
I can never feel
at ease with anymore:

remember where you've been, and why.
And then build houses; build villages,
dikes and schools, songs
and children in that green land
I blackened with my shadow
and the shadow of my flag.

Remember Ho Chi Minh
was a poet: please,
do not let it all come down
to nothing.


# Leaving the Guns Behind

Light sails west;
night sails in across the Eastern Shore;
we sail south past Turkey Point
where colonial gunrunners anchored.

We sail south past Aberdeen,
where the modern merchants
test their latest wares;
past Georgetown, where the lady
loaded cannon with the troops;
past Baltimore, where the British navy
burst bombs in air.

We sail south past Annapolis;
past the river of the eastern Union army,
where the Pentagon squats;
past St. Michaels, where the hunters
manned their duck-blinds with artillery.

Night sails on, and we sail south
past Norfolk navy yard
toward open sea
and bellies full of Caribbean rum,
toward always-sun and always-willing
nut-brown women
old Cornwallis dreamed of in the night
before the morning he surrendered.

# After the Fire

After the fire
burns out,
and the stillness
sweeps in, we
begin to observe
small things: red
welts, slight
bruises on
pubic bones, musky
impatience of wet lace—Oh, my
face in your
breasts, and
yours in my
hair, and the
laughter
softly lapping the night
like a sea.


# Twodot, Montana

I knew that Sunday morning
only what I could see: dust
dancing in waves on a single unpaved street,
swirling in tiny plumes, unswirling,
blowing away through summer heat; two cats
asleep on a windowledge; a dog asleep
on the street in the shade of the plank sidewalk;
squat frame buildings, half of them boarded shut.
I had followed Mac's directions perfectly;
this had to be Twodot—but I was lost.
Out of the car, I gingerly looked in windows:
peer in the barbershop-post office—nobody there;
peer in the Twodot Bar, where Saturday nights
the cowhands wash down whole weeks
of prairie dust—nobody there either.
At one end of town, the railroad station seemed
to collapse board by board as I watched, the train
coming once a year, loading cattle for slaughter.

Beyond the last buildings, a few small silver
Airstream Specials crouched, bolted to concrete
foundations against Canadian winter winds,
space between them for kitchen gardens.
A woman there answered my question:
on down the road ten more miles; Mary and Pete's
would be the Big House, the first one; the 'boy,'
Mac, lived in the Little House beyond that.
Clawing dry earth with a hoe as she talked, hair
stiff and pale as dry prairie grass, her eyes
fell back inside themselves like old volcanoes
or the insides of empty whiskey bottles,
something deep within resenting the intrusion
of people who come and go when they please.
I got in the car and left, thinking that morning,
"perhaps because it's Sunday."


## Welcome

When you have ridden once too often
jostling on the El
in a crowd at dusk with no one
to talk to, and no one
waiting at home;

when you have eaten your last meal
alone;

when you have said your final
hello to the grocer
in that same strange voice
like a cry;

when you have given up hope
ever of turning the next corner
to find the door
with no lock, and a lamp
burning on the other side;

you will come to the door
with no lock
and no lamp,

and you will open it.

Come in;
sit down, rest, and eat.
See: we have saved you a place
at our table.

# The Spiders' White Dream of Peace

I've had nightmares before—this
wasn't an ordinary
nightmare that jerks you awake
at the last second, startled
but free—this was something else:
it was spiders telling their
secrets in my ear, at night,
alone with them in my bed—
I wasn't even asleep.
There were hundreds of them, all
crowding around me, crawling
on top of one another,
each trying to be the one—
be the first one—to tell me
their whole plan. It was easy
to see they wanted to please
me; I couldn't understand
why. They knew what we needed—
I couldn't believe it—I
tried to wake up; I couldn't.
They were plotting the end of
the world: together they would
rise up, rise as one army
of weavers, together spin
their delicate webs back and
forth, under and over, wrap
the whole earth in a cocoon
and leave it hanging in space—
a soft white ball forever
silent, preserved, without want.

# Empire

I. Barbarian tribesmen
   stand in the light
   still on the crests of the hills.
   They shake their weapons in the air,
   gesture lewdly, and jeer
   at the soldiers in the valley
   where the watchfires
   flicker at the rising shadows.

   Down below, Roman officers
   drink wine and plan;
   soldiers tug cloaks
   more tightly around their shoulders,
   mutter about the food,
   and think of wives and lovers
   as the sentries take their posts
   around the camp: a circle of eyes
   peering into the darkness
   at the edge of the empire.

II. In Perkasie and Pittsburgh,
    North Platte, Grosse Point and Portland,
    Memorial Day crowds line the streets
    cheering for the local high school band.
    The majorettes are beautiful
    and young;
    and the solemn Legionnaires, young
    thirty years ago, fire
    fake bullets for the dead.
    Picnics follow in the afternoon,
    and all across America
    swimming pools open for the summer.

    The honored dead are white,
    or died
    trying to be white,
    red and blue: there are
    no twenty-one-gun salutes
    for Crazy Horse.

On this day, in 1431,
Joan of Arc was burned to death
by the English
and the Catholic Church.
She died for France.

III. When the dinosaurs died,
dim-witted and without complaint,
they left behind
a noble silence,
and a world
still capable of life.

IV. The great auks
and the passenger pigeons
are gone forever;
the gorillas are in Lincoln Park Zoo.
The redwood trees, poking
into the clouds already when Christ
calmed the turbulent waters of Galilee,
are picket fences in Daly City.
The whales—greys and blues, fins,
humps and pilots—breaching for air, find
only the patient harpooneers' exploding barbs
while the whooping cranes sail south
each year in smaller numbers,
their nesting grounds
along the Texas Gulf of Mexico
cities now, and refineries.
The bald eagles die
unhatched in their eggs;
the dolphins die in the tunamen's nets.

V. Toward the end, they understood
it was no use
complaining: they began to pray,
truly believing their prayers
and in the God they prayed to,
calling each other
sister and brother, sharing
what food and shelter they could find.

In the darkness when they died,
they were alone.

# A Confirmation

**for Gerry Gaffney**

Solemn Douglas firs stride slowly
down steep hills to drink
the waters of the wild Upper Umqua.
In a small clearing in the small
carved ravine of a feeder stream
we camp, pitching our tent
in the perfect stillness of the shadows
of the Klamath Indians. Far off,
almost in a dream, the logging trucks
growl west down through the mountains
toward the mills in Roseburg.

I hold the stakes, you hammer:
"Watch the fingers!"—both laughing.
Both recall, in easy conversation,
one-man poncho-tents rigged
side by side in total darkness,
always you and I, in iron heat,
in the iron monsoon rains—
not like this at all; and yet,
though years have passed
and we are older by a lifetime,
a simple slip of thought, a pause,
and here: nothing's changed.

For we were never young, it seems;
not then, or ever. I couldn't even cry
the day you went down screaming, angry
jagged steel imbedded in your knee—
I knew you would live,
and I knew you wouldn't be back,
and I was glad, and a little jealous.
Two months later I went down.

We all went down eventually,
the villages aflame, the long
grim lines of soldiers, flotsam
in the vortex of a sinking illusion:
goodbye, Ginny; goodbye, John Kennedy;
goodbye, Tom Paine and high school history—
though here we are still, you and I.
We live our lives now
in a kind of awkward silence
in the perfect stillness of the shadows
of the Klamath Indians.

And I am truly happy
to be with you again. We stand
on the rocks; you point to clear
patches between white water
where the shadows of sleek fish slip,
effortless streaks of energy.
I'm clumsy: with an old, eager patience
you teach me how to cast the fly
gently, so it rides on the surface
with the current, far downstream—
till the rod bends, springs back,
bends again: strike! Your excitement
rises above the river like a wild
song the Douglas firs bend
imperceptibly to hear: shouts,
advice, encouragement, half an hour
and a fourteen-inch rainbow trout
panting hard, eyes alive, its tiny heart
beating with defiance still unbroken
though I hold the fish
helpless in my hands.

I throw the fish back
in the awkward silence, and you
slip your arm around my shoulders
gently for a moment, knowing why.

Later we eat from cans,
the rainbow flashing in the fire
reflecting in our eyes, alive:

familiar gestures—fingers burned
by hot tin lids, a mild curse, quiet
laughter, swish of a knifeblade
plunging idly deep into damp earth.
You ask do I remember the little shy
flower who always wore a white Ao Dai,
and I smile across the flames as the river
tumbles through the darkness toward the sea
that laps the shores of Asia.

The wind moves through the Douglas firs,
and in the perfect stillness of the shadows
of the Klamath Indians, we test
our bonds and find them, after all
these years, still sound—knowing
in the awkward silence we will always share
something worth clinging to
out of the permanent past of stillborn dreams:
the ancient, implacable wisdom
of ignorance shattered forever, a new
reverence we were never taught
by anyone we believed, a frail hope
we gave each other, communion
made holy by our shame.

You've found religion since then,
a wife, and two children;
I write poems you admire.
The knee's still stiff, like an old
high school football wound,
and I have trouble hearing. We are
both tired, but reluctant to sleep:
both understand we will never
see each other again; once is enough.
The logging trucks have long since
left the mountains in peace;
in the perfect stillness, we can almost
hear the solemn Douglas firs drinking
the waters of the wild Upper Umqua
we have come so far to worship:
together now, in this small circle of light,
we bow our hearts to the shadows
of the Klamath Indians; now,
and always, in our need.

## Waking Alone in Darkness

It's only the wind, mothers
tell their children in the night
when upturned leaves rattle on the windowpanes,
furious and black;

only the wind
when night cries in children's dreams,
and children cry out
in the darkness.

# Peary & Henson Reach the North Pole

Donaldo, Stephen and I
started out at dusk as light
snow fell from scudding clouds
in the middle of the coldest
winter in the history of Chicago.

Along the lake, mounds of ice
obscured the shoreline; we trudged
in silence where it should have been,
across those wind-carved crests frozen
in the final act of breaking.

North and east, through failing light,
great jagged dragons' teeth of ice
reared up in broken rows;
and farther out, the white
horizon lumbered into night.

We could have walked through
falling snow and glowing darkness
over ice all the way to Mackinac
had we been bold enough,
equipped, and slightly mad;

but we turned back finally
because Kathleen was waiting
with hot rum in a warm apartment,
because our jobs were waiting in the morning,

and because, for most of us,
it is enough to feel the blind
brute hammer of the earth
beating toward the limits of endurance
only for a moment.

# Turning Thirty

It isn't that I fear
growing older—such things as fear,
reluctance or desire
play no part at all
except as light and shadow sweep a hillside
on a Sunday afternoon,
astonishing the eye but passing on
at sunset with the land
still unchanged: the same rocks,
the same trees, tall grass gently drifting—
merely that I do not understand
how my age has come to me,
or what it means.

It's almost like some small
forest creature one might find
outside the door some frosty autumn morning,
tired, lame, uncomprehending,
almost calm.
You want to stroke its fur,
pick it up, mend the leg and send it
scampering away—but something
in its eyes says, "no;
this is how I live, and how I die."
And so, a little sad, you let it be.
Later when you look,
the thing is gone.

And just like that these
thirty years have come and gone;
and I do not understand at all
why I see a man
inside the mirror when a small
boy still lives inside this body
wondering
what causes laughter, why
nations go to war, who paints the startling
colors of the rainbow on a gray vaulted sky,
and when I will be old enough
to know.

# The Teacher

**for my students at Sandy Spring**
**Friends School; September, 1978**

A cold moon hangs
cold fire among the clouds,
and I remember colder nights
in hell when men died
in such pale light as this
of fire swift
and deadly as a heart of ice.

Hardly older then
than you are now,
I hunched down shaking
like an old man
alone in an empty cave
among the rocks of ignorance
and malice honorable men
call truth.

Out of that cave I carried
anger like a torch
to keep my heart from freezing,
and a strange new thing called
love
to keep me sane.

A dozen years ago,
before I ever knew you,
beneath a moon not unlike
this moon tonight,
I swore an oath to teach you
all I know—
and I know things
worth knowing.

It is a desperate future
I cling to,
and it is yours.
All that I have lived for
since that cold moon long ago
hangs in the balance—
and I keep fumbling for words,
but this clip-clapper tongue
won't do.

I am afraid;
I do not want to fail:

I need your hands to steady me;
I need your hearts to give me courage;
I need you to walk with me in silence
until I find a voice that speaks
the language
that you speak.

# Companions

Older than ancient, you shadow me
like some puzzled persistent companion.
Wherever I go, whatever I do,
you are there gazing over my shoulder
wide-eyed, bent forward from the hips,
your broad brows furrowed in thought,
long arms gently swaying.

The simplest things amaze you:
when I eat with a fork, your hands
open and close in clumsy imitation;
when I pull on my boots, you
paw at them softly, rocking
back on your haunches, wide lips
stretched in a kind of grin;
you ride in the back seat of my car
terrified, cowering down in a corner.

Yet you swing from the branches of trees
graceful and light as a cat, scampering
over the earth swiftly, agile, alert
to every sound and odor on the wind.
You understand fire, pointing in awe
to the thin flames of hot light,
prodding the coals with a stick,
chattering explanations in your
strange gutteral tongue.

You mourn for the dead;
I have heard your heartbroken howl
piercing the night beneath the new moon.
You know what it means to be lonely.

Feeling the undefinable pull
of the dark centuries rising between us
like tides, you huddle inside your cave
with the small fire leaping against the walls
and the glowing eyes of jackels
dotting the black mouth like stars.
The young burrow deeply into your fur.
On the threshold of sleep, you peer
far into the night, awaiting the first
signs of light in the eastern sky—
and I am the bright gleam leaping
deep in your eyes.

# Last of the Hard-hearted Ladies

I was always afraid of you—
other grandmothers lovingly
baked pies for grandchildren;
you kicked my ass
for leaving socks on the floor:
it made no sense—

until that day, fifteen,
and no one home but you,
I asked you for a cigarette;
and you said yes,
and talked with me all afternoon
as though I were a man,
and never told a soul.

Years later, I understood
you'd simply always seen the man
leaving socks on the floor
and coats on chairs; and all
you'd ever asked
is that I see it too.

Oh, you bitched about my hair
and my moustache, never liked
my politics: that socialistic crap—
but you grinned like the devil
when I held my ground:
you liked backbone.

I didn't say a word today
when Dad and Uncle Merv
read that stuff from the Bible
you'd scoffed at all your life,
remembering the times we'd sat
listening to the hymns in church
next door, smoking cigarettes:

they think their faith will help you,
and maybe it will; and anyway,
it can't hurt—and the grief,
at least, is real.

So don't be angry with me, Grandma:
if I'd had it our way,
I'd have lit up another cigarette
and passed it to you.

# Lost at Sea
## Green Turtle Cay, Bahamas

In the language of people,
there is no word for this moment:
as you lie sleeping, the sun breaks
over the rim of the New World,
and an east wind shimmers the sea
white over a dozen shades of blue.
Offshore, where the waves break
over the reefs, the broken hulls
of old ships lie crusted with coral.

Watching the rhythm of life
beating beneath soft breasts falling
and rising through the stillness
of your dreams, I imagine
men on the deck of a ship
within sight of trees on a white beach
after the long passage west.

Will we ever return
to the safety of familiar places
where channels are marked by lights
and bells signal shoal water?
Did the men whose bones lie
there beneath the sea beyond the window
cry out loud in the last moment
as the ship went down?

The sun pours color over your face,
and I stroke your tangled hair,
feeling the pull of warm lands
beyond familiar northern seas, knowing
at least a few of those sailors
went down in silence, content.

# Sunset

## Dresden Nuclear Power Station, Morris, Illinois

Late afternoon: in the stillness
before evening, a car on the road
between cornfields surrounding
Dresden Station raises a plume
of dust, and a light wind
settles the dust gently over the corn.
Power lines over the cornfields
audibly sing the power of cities
beyond sight, where neon lights flash
tomorrow, laughter and dreams.
Deep within Dresden Station,
human beings tamper with atoms.

Dresden: say it, and the air
fills with the wail of sirens,
thin fingers of light
frantically probing the clouds,
red bursting anger, black thunder,
the steel drone of the heavy bombers,
dry bones rattle of falling bombs:
    deliver us from fire;
    deliver us from the flames;
    Lord, have mercy upon us.
135,000 human beings
died in the flames of Dresden.

The air to the west is on fire.
The lake to the west burns red
with the sun's descending fire.
The sky rises out of the lake gold
to copper to deep blue, falling
gently away, black, to the east.
Deep within Dresden Station,
human beings tamper with atoms.
Light wind rustles the cornstalks,
the sound like the rustle of skirts
on young graceful women.

## Again, Rehoboth

I have stood by this bay before.
I have watched the light from the moon
dance in the eyes of friends
while the moon danced on black water;
wanting to know where you were,
exactly what you were thinking.

There was a time when I thought
a man could suffocate
in the dark abscess of want;
a time when I didn't believe
tomorrow would come
except in the shape I gave it.

You belong to that time—you
and the tears that fell in the wake
of the false peace of October
when it still seemed possible
to wield light like a sword.

I am a teacher now;
I live alone.
I am anchored to this world
by all cold necessity
holds sacred: water, salt,
the labored rhythms of breathing.

I cherish my friends,
whose thin threads spread like glowing wires
out from the center, bending away
over the four horizons
in smooth unbroken lines,
and the quiet slap of the water
kissing the land.

When did the recognition come—
the slow submission of dreams; the wind
turning to blow down the years
like a steady silence—
things seem hardly to have changed
at all: these hands; this head
with its wild brown mane;
this heart still beating.

Evening approaches; already
the first star burns in the east.
There will be no moon tonight.
Out on the bay, the boats beat home
to the seagulls' plaintive cries,
their smooth bending sails
blood-red from a fire sun.

# Fog

Snow all night; and then the temperature
up fifteen degrees before dawn:
white slush, wet sludge beneath,
not fit for anything—not even children;
and the fog curtaining up from the ground
luminous, so thick you have to part it
as you walk, and duck quickly
under branches out of nowhere.
You know today the sun is shining
somewhere, but it isn't here.

Here, the day is wrapped tightly
in a white shroud shivering thoughts
out of places no one ever visits
on an ordinary day, though admission price
is cheap and never varies:
*see yourself the way you really are*—
the way, at least, light bent through fog
makes you seem when all reassurances
are gone, it's Sunday, you live alone,
and even the telephone won't ring. Funny

how the good seems nebulous as fog.
Wrong ways, wrong words, wrong decisions
hammer like a blacksmith on an anvil:
people you will never see again come back
real as people you will have to face tomorrow—
and if you've done it wrong, you've done it
wrong so many times it hurts to be alone
on days like this with thirty years of flaws
and nothing in the house but bourbon.

A long, very long day. Well,
it's good bourbon in any case; and it's
evening now. Snow and mud are freezing;
fog is lifting: clear sky, perhaps,
by morning. So you go to sleep
listening to the silence broken
only by the hammer, waiting
for an ordinary day to set you straight.

# The Eruption of Mount St. Helens

**for Nimimosha of the Bear Tribe**
**Medicine Society**

"Ash fallout is the hot news here."
Too far away to feel or hear the blast,
Nimimosha watched the gray-brown cloud
rising and advancing east
until the land and all living things
lay blanketed in ash, and her daughter's
infant eyes burned red with grit;
then she went inside.

"If it rains lightly now," she writes,
"the ash will turn to caustic paste
and harden to dissolve slowly,
burning the earth as it goes.
We're concerned about the fish"—
jellied mud on surfaces of ponds
and lakes, blocking oxygen exchange;
"the cows are eating ash-coated grass,
drinking ash-coated water,
blinking ash-coated eyes.
Then there are the horses. . . .

"We must stay inside.
The highways all around Spokane
are blocked; telephones are down;
everything is closed. We're thankful

"things are not too bad; even though
the day turned black at noon, the world
continues, and we're all still here.
The feeling here is powerful.
Walk in balance on Mother Earth."

My ash-coated heart soars
to where she is—as if desire alone
could lift the burden of her hardship,
clean the water, feed the cows, wipe
the burning grit from Yarroe's eyes—
and yet I cannot cry:

Nature's fury lacks the malice
of seashore wildlife sanctuaries
smothering in oil from sinking tankers,
or an Indochinése village disappearing
in an orange ball of napalm, or a lake
dying from the mills in Buffalo,
or the slums of Baltimore.

I will not cry for Nimimosha:
St. Helens is the throat of Mother Earth,
and the violence is Her song—
and there is no sadness in it.

# Matters of the Heart
### for Thomas McGrath & James Cooney

Old Tom, your rasping low voice
is so soft it's hard to imagine machinegun
bullets among the strikers in New Orleans
or the hard clubs on soft round heads
by the docks in New York City;
Jim, shuffling along with your walking stick
like an angry shepherd, kind as a good Samaritan,
first American printer of Miller and Nin:

"The deepest part of a man is his sense
of essential truth, essential honour, essential
justice: they hated him because he was free,
because he wasn't cowed as they were . . ."

"Wild talk, and easy enough now to laugh.
*That's* not the point and never was the point:
What was real was the generosity, expectant hope.
The open and true desire to create the good."

You rascals. What am I supposed to do?
Storm the White House? Picket Chase Manhattan?
What? I've tried it all, believe me; nothing
works. Everyone's asleep, or much too busy.

The point is: things are different now.
In the age of the MX missile and the Trident
nuclear submarine and the 20-megaton bomb
multiplied by a couple of thousand or so,
what are the odds I'll ever see
the same age you are now?

Did it seem so bleak in 1940
in that awful twilight when half the world
plunged headlong into darkness
out of the decade of comradeship and hope
while the other half stood poised to follow?

Four more decades have passed since then,
and you're still at it. The Pole Star's gone;
even the dreams we steered by only ten years ago
are gone. Where do you get your strength?

I'm tired of being swatted like a bothersome fly:
pariah, voice in the wilderness. My friends
look at me with pity in their eyes.
I want to own a house, raise a family,
draw a steady paycheck. What, after all, can I do
to change the course of a whole mad world?
I'm only a man; I want to forget for awhile
and be happy . . .
                    . . . and yet your lives,
your words, your breath, your beating
old tired fighters' unbowed hearts
boom through the stillness of excuses
like a stuck clock forever tolling:

"Don't give in. Go on. Keep on.
Resist. Keep on. Go on."

# Briana

### for CJ, in memory of Jill

Death comes knocking and silence descends
like a black bird alighting on the windowledge
on a black night with no candles.

Yet everything continues: bottle time,
nap time, play time, bath time, story time,
bed time—only a brief confusion:
for a few days you asked for mommy;
then you stopped asking.

You can't know the black bird will sit
for a lifetime in your father's heart.
I watch him with you now:
the tall slender frame
bending over your crib like a willow;
the large hands hesitantly poised—
wanting to touch,
not wanting to wake you;
the soft searching eyes permanently puzzling
an incomprehensible absence
he will never let you feel
if he can help it.

Years will pass before you understand
the secret tremble when your father holds you,
just how much such a small child weighs—
but that's okay;
                don't trouble your dreams
with wondering. Be what you are:
your mother's daughter. Be a candle.

Light the awful silence with your laughter.

## Yours

So now it has come to this:
through dark tunnels, arm-in-arm,
the damp walls cracked
and echoing our footsteps;
on past highways paved
with the harbor of night,
where the sound of tires,
though close, is now intangible,
like unseen ships along the Delaware
whose foghorns conjure
worlds of ice, exotic markets,
lions on a beach;
or rails that hum
with melancholy travelers
miles to the east;

through the shadows of trees,
and branches startling in the dark,
and cold wet grass;
past buildings swallowed by the hour,
empty of all but dreams;
on, and still on
to an old stone bench
carved at the edge of a wood
where we sit and shiver together,
reluctant, but unable to return.

Yes, it has come to an old stone bench,
and to an end of an old life
in an older, simpler world,
and to a harsh
yet undeniably desired
awakening.

# Channel Fever

When I cast off in my small boat
with its one sail white and yellow
brilliant in the sunlight, I thought
I heard the sea calling in a soft song
sweet as any mermaid sings to sailors
in their dreams. I disappeared after it
into that vastness searching, searching.

I have caught fish to feed myself,
throwing the offal and bones to the sharks,
eating the meat raw, washing it down
with rainwater collected in a tin cup.

I never imagined it would be so lonely.
At times I have been delirious:
tearing the tattered remnants of my clothes,
shouting at stars, fighting to keep
from pitching myself headlong into the sea.

The dolphins, at least, were real; sometimes
on bright days they paced my small boat,
breasting the waves, laughing—or at night,
their sleek gray bodies luminescent green
in phosphorescent moonlight. For awhile,
I thought it was their song I followed—
but the wind blew too steady for that;
the wind drove my small boat always
over the next wave, and over the next wave.

When I first smelled land, I didn't believe it.
"Is this what it means to be mad?" I thought.
But my small boat surged suddenly forward,
and the seabirds riding the waves suddenly
surged up screaming and whirling in great
wheeling circles of excitement—and I know now,
as any sailor does even before the long voyage

is over, all along it was your
invisible hand on the tiller, your
breath beating my small boat steadily on
toward the harbor shaped like a heart.
It was you.
It is your song I heard.

## The Reason Why

In Russia, everyone drinks vodka.
They all wear furry hats, and worship
at the tomb of Lenin. Godless,
every last one of them, and hell-bent
on conquering the world. Yesterday
Afghanistan; today Nicaragua; tomorrow
New Jersey. Atlantic City! Sweet
Jesus, all those elegant casinos
in the hands of Reds. That's why
we need missiles. MX missiles.
Cruise missiles. Pershing missiles.
Let'em try to take the Boardwalk;
we'll blow their godless hats off.

# The Suicide

That winter the woman hurled herself
under the Bethlehem Local,
I was ten. Understand: in Perkasie,
no one had died for years
of anything but old age and heart attacks;
maybe an auto accident now and then;
sensible causes even a child could grasp.

That winter I walked the tracks a dozen times
looking for clues:
dried blood, shredded clothing, flesh;
trying hard to imagine screaming
steel wheels clawing at steel rails
and the inconceivable thump
of deliberate death.


# Moments When the World Consents

Atlantic waves roil over reefs beyond the cut
between Tooloo and Elbow Cays, boom
and boom on jagged coral, disintegrating
skyward in repeating crystal spray.
A quarter-mile away, behind the windward cays,
Abaco Sound lies blue on gently rippling
blue, and in the islands' lees, wild peas
and bougainvillaea blossom under Caribbean pines.

You lie face down; I watch the water
in the shallow sheltered cove we've come to share.
Warm wind in coconut palms along the beach
seems to set the broad green leaves to talking
softly : "Stay awhile, you two, be still;
this hour, this afternoon, this day; be
jealous of the moments when the world
consents to give you to each other
undistracted. You may not find another place
or time to smell good air blown all the way
from Africa or Spain, or lie on sand so
smooth and white and warm and meant
for you."

I let my fingers fall across your hips.
You turn, and open like a flower.
Love, like sun-warmed swirling tiny pearl waves
on satin water, laps our naked thighs.


# Deer

Two white-tailed deer stood still
on George School's South Lawn
not fifty yards away from where we jogged.
My wife said, "Look," and as she did,
they both looked too, then bounded off
across the lawn, white tails flying.
We jogged on in silence, thinking
of their perfect strides, their grace,
their quick flight at our approach.

Two nights later, my wife came home
in tears—a rainy night, unseasonably
warm, foggy—she'd almost struck a deer
already lying on the highway,
had stopped the car just in time
and gotten out to find it
not yet dead: at her approach,
it kicked its mangled legs, convulsed,
and tried to rise as if to run, fell back,
tried again and fell, and tried, and fell.

I thought of the deer on South Lawn:
their perfect strides; their grace;
their quick flight at our approach,
as if they thought we meant
to do them harm.

# Letter to the Survivors

To any who find this,
understand:

year by year, we could see it
approaching—the tensions
mounting, the missiles
mounting, the bombers
rising, the submarines slipping
down their long thin launch-ramp rails,
the warheads, and multiple warheads.
We knew it,
but we were afraid.
We were ordinary people, only
the work-a-day Marys and Joes.
Our leaders insisted
they were striving for peace.
What could we do
but believe them?
We had only our one vote each,
only our small voices;
and it was a crime to refuse
to serve, and a crime
to refuse to pay.
We did not want to lose our friends;
we did not want to lose our jobs;
we did not want to lose our homes—

and we didn't really believe
it could happen.

# The Invasion of Grenada

I didn't want a monument,
not even one as sober as that
vast black wall of broken lives.
I didn't want a postage stamp.
I didn't want a road beside the Delaware
River with a sign proclaiming:
"Vietnam Veterans Memorial Highway."

What I wanted was a simple recognition
of the limits of our power as a nation
to inflict our will on others.
What I wanted was an understanding
that the world is neither black-and-white
nor ours.
What I wanted was an end to monuments.

But no one
ever asked me what I wanted.

# High Country

Brad pitched the tent beside the creek
among the hummingbirds below the beaver
dam where the water flowed swiftly,
and whenever we wanted we could dip
our tin cups into the creek and drink.
For three days we lived on rainbow trout,
and at night the stars were so close
we climbed the Milky Way with our dreams
and stalked the Bear with Orion.

We were twenty-three. The world
6000 feet below swept out across
the compass points like a storm.
Our Asian war staggered on; calculating
men in three-piece suits and uniforms
with stars called firestorms down upon
the heads of people with conical hats
and spoke of Peace with Honor.
But up in the high country, life
went on with only a brief intrusion,
once, of contrails knifing the sky.

Time since then has driven a wedge
of ten years and 2000 miles between us.
Brad's a surgeon in Madison; I teach
in a Quaker boarding school in the east.
Calculating men in three-piece suits
and uniforms with stars are calling down
firestorms upon the heads of peasants
in Central America now. I often think
of plunging into the icy creek at dawn,
of the water rushing among the rocks,
and over our bodies, and on.

# About the Author

W. D. Ehrhart was born in 1948 and grew up in Perkasie, Pennsylvania. He holds a BA from Swarthmore College and an MA from the University of Illinois at Chicago. He currently lives in Doylestown, PA, with his wife, Anne.

Ehrhart enlisted in the U.S. Marines in 1966, serving in Vietnam and receiving an honorable discharge. He later became active with Vietnam Veterans Against the War, contributing poetry to the 1972 anthology, *Winning Hearts and Minds.*

Ehrhart's prose and poetry have since appeared in numerous periodicals and anthologies including *Another Chicago Magazine, The Virginia Quarterly Review, New Letters, TriQuarterly, The Greenfield Review, The Chronicle of Higher Education, From A to Z: 200 Contemporary American Poets, Leaving the Bough: 50 American Poets of the 80's,* and *Peace Is Our Profession.*

Ehrhart was featured in Episode 5 of the recent PBS documentary, *Vietnam : A Television History,* and is one of only two poets represented in the companion book, *Vietnam: An Anthology and Guide to a Television History.*

# Other books by W. D. Ehrhart

Poetry:
*The Outer Banks and Other Poems*, Adastra Press

Prose:
*Vietnam-Perkasie*, McFarland & Company

As co-editor:
*Demilitarized Zones*, East River Anthology

As contributing editor:
*Those Who Were There*, Dustbooks

# Other Books from Thunder's Mouth Press

*The Red Menace* Michael Anania
*Coagulations; New and Selected Poems* Jayne Cortez
*She Had Some Horses* Joy Harjo
*Dos Indios* Harold Jaffe
*America Made Me* Hans Koning
*When the Revolution Really* Peter Michelson
*Echoes Inside the Labyrinth* Thomas McGrath
*Fightin'* Simon J. Ortiz
*From Sand Creek* Simon J. Ortiz
*The Mojo Hands Call/I Must Go* Sterling Plumpp
*Somehow We Survive* Sterling Plumpp (ed.)


Write for a complete catalog: TMP, Box 780, NYC, 10025

811.54      Eh8t      60-89

Ehrhart

TO THOSE WHO HAVE GONE HOME TIRED

## DATE DUE

|  |  |  |  |
|---|---|---|---|
|  |  |  |  |
|  |  |  |  |
|  |  |  |  |
|  |  |  |  |
|  |  |  |  |
|  |  |  |  |
|  |  |  |  |
|  |  |  |  |
|  |  |  |  |
|  |  |  |  |
|  |  |  |  |
|  |  |  |  |